Trace & Learn

DINOSAUR
Handwriting Practice

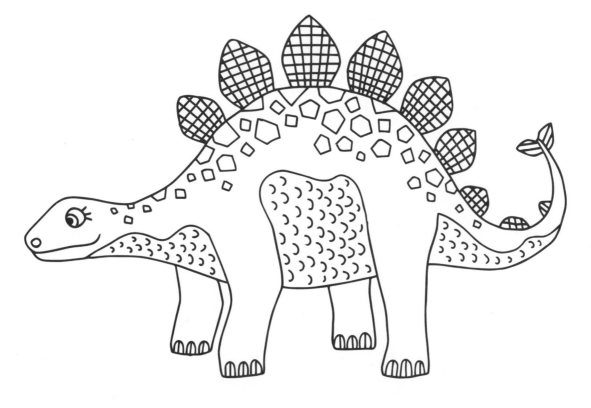

Text: Elizabeth Golding
Illustrations: Lisa Mallett
Design: Anton Poitier

iseek

My name is

_____

_____

I like

dinosaurs

Help your child to develop handwriting skills

Use this book to encourage your child to learn the letters of the alphabet and practice their handwriting skills, using both UPPERCASE and lowercase letters. This book is typeset in Sassoon, a typeface developed by Rosemary Sassoon after researching what letterforms children found easiest to read. This typeface is widely used in schools to teach reading and handwriting.

Here are the main handwriting styles that are typically taught:
Print: The letters do not join and have various start and finish points for each letter.
Cursive: The letters have starting points in print, but exit strokes, or tails, are also included.
Continuous cursive: The letters are joined together in a continuous flow of connected writing.

In Sassoon lowercase letterforms, the exit strokes link together visually, making an understandable link from print to continuous cursive writing.

This book uses a dinosaur theme to motivate early readers. There are lots of pictures, which you can use to encourage your child to color after tracing and copying the letters.

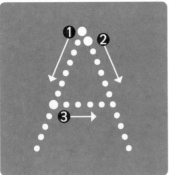

A is for Apple

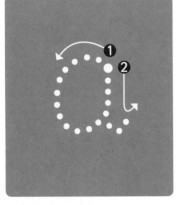

a is in hot

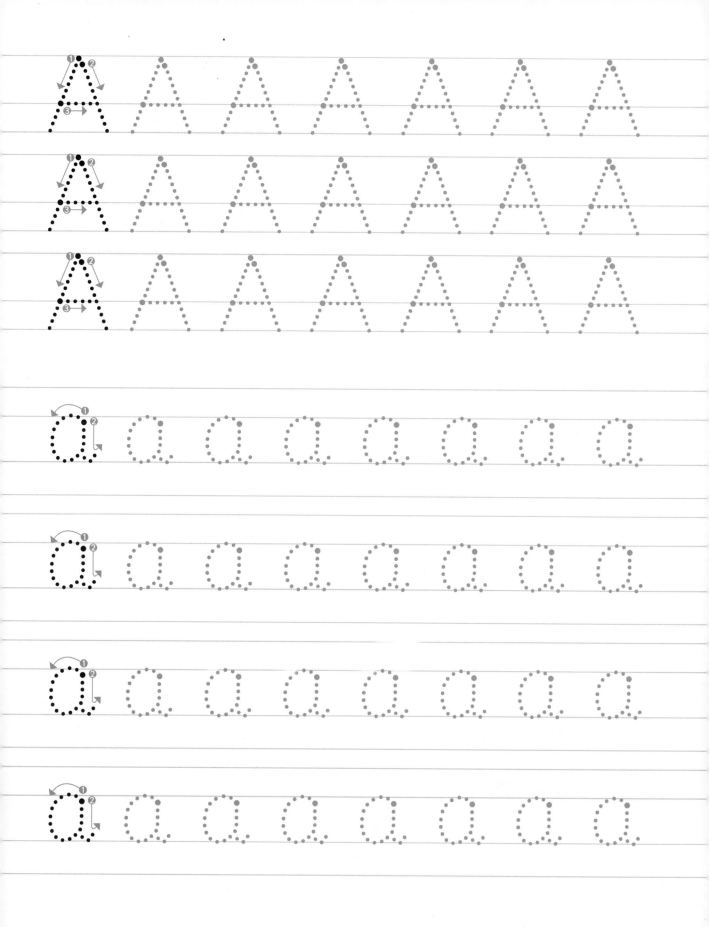

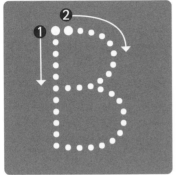

B is for Butterfly

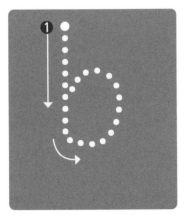

b is in crab

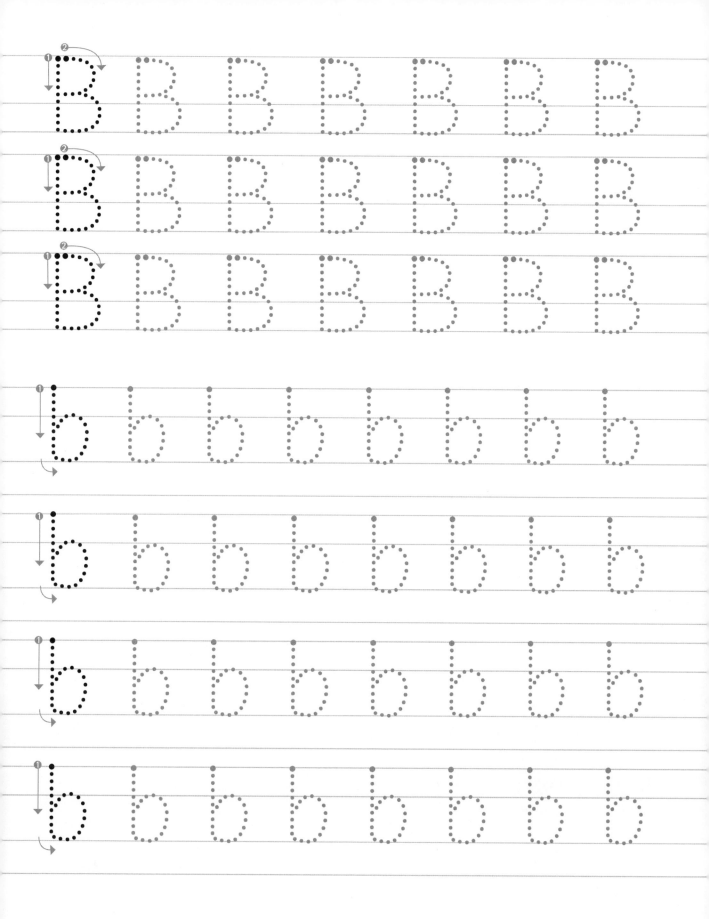

C is for Cat

c is in duck

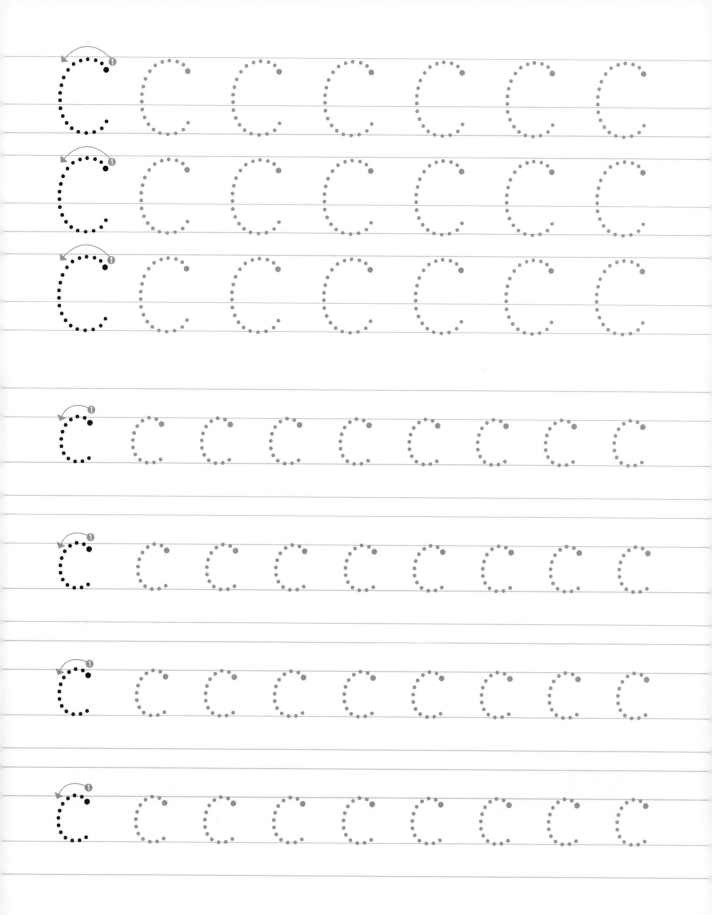

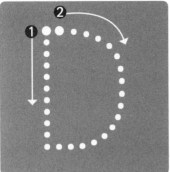

D is for Dog

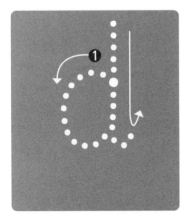

d is in bed

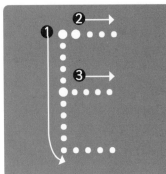

E is for Elephant

e is in hen

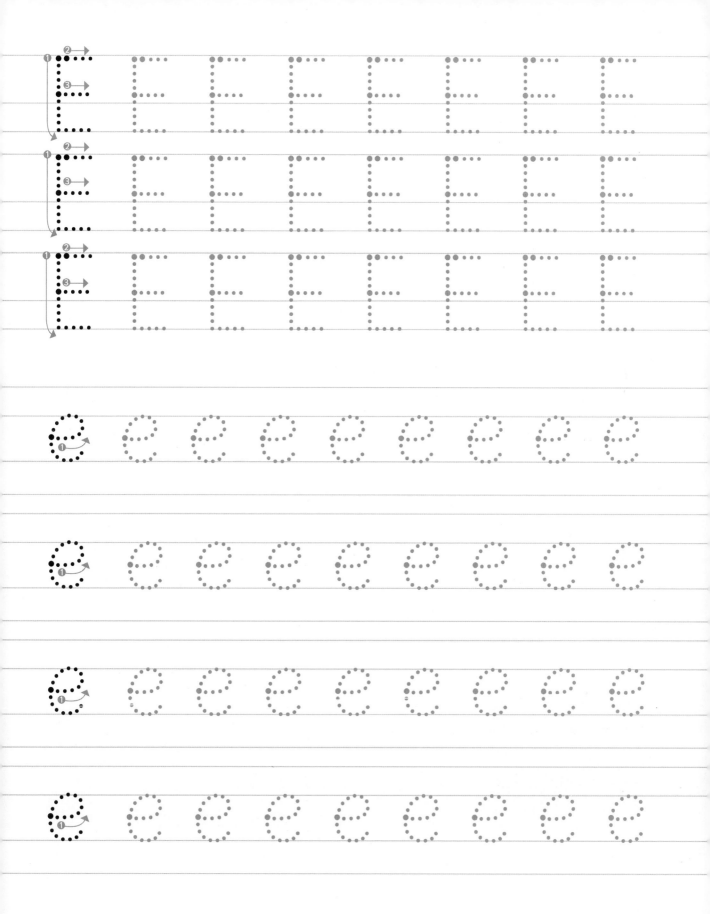

F is for Frog

f is in butterfly

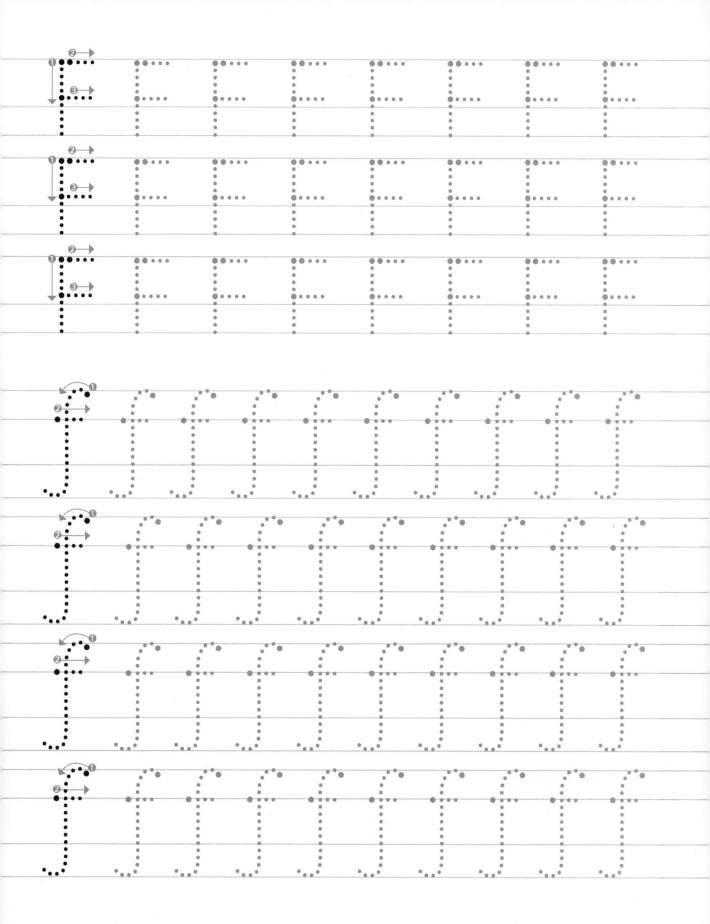

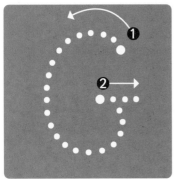

G is for Giraffe

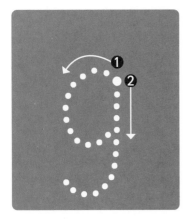

g is in frog

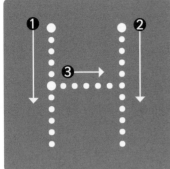

H is for Hippo

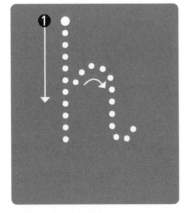

h is in fish

H H H H H H H H H H

H H H H H H H H H H

H H H H H H H H H H

h h h h h h h h h

h h h h h h h h h

h h h h h h h h h

h h h h h h h h h

I is for Ink

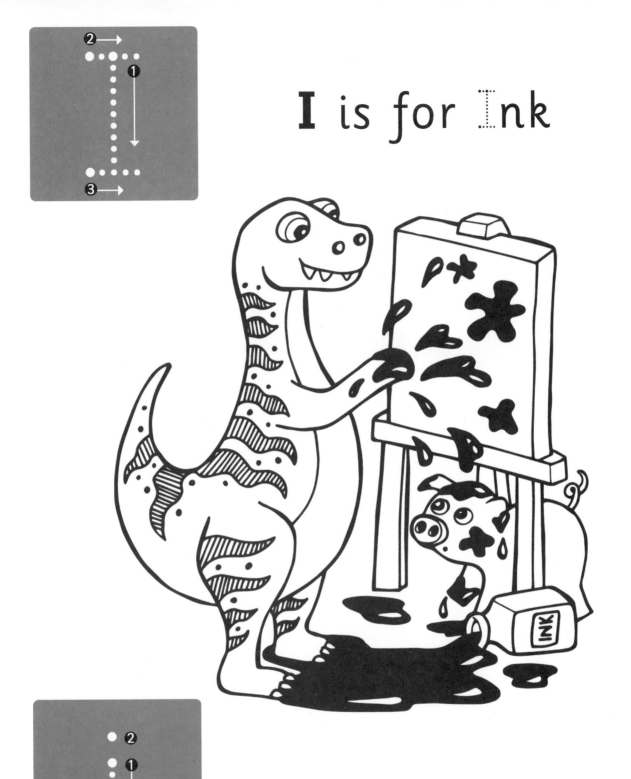

i is in pig

I I I I I I I I I I

I I I I I I I I I I

I I I I I I I I I I

i i i i i i i i i i i

i i i i i i i i i i i

i i i i i i i i i i i

i i i i i i i i i i i

J is for Jelly

j is in pajamas

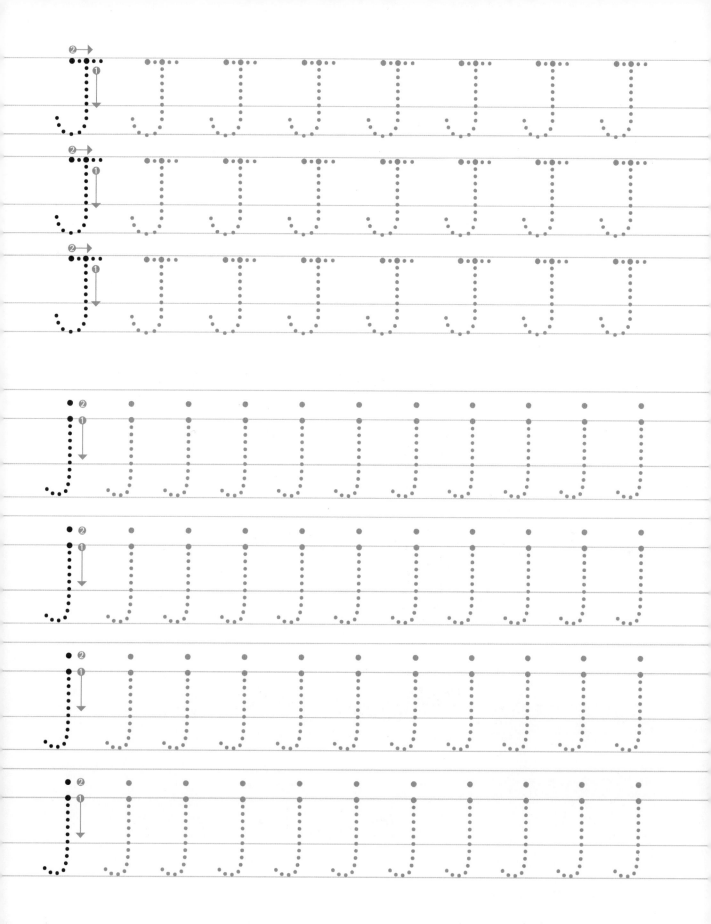

K is for Koala

k is in cake

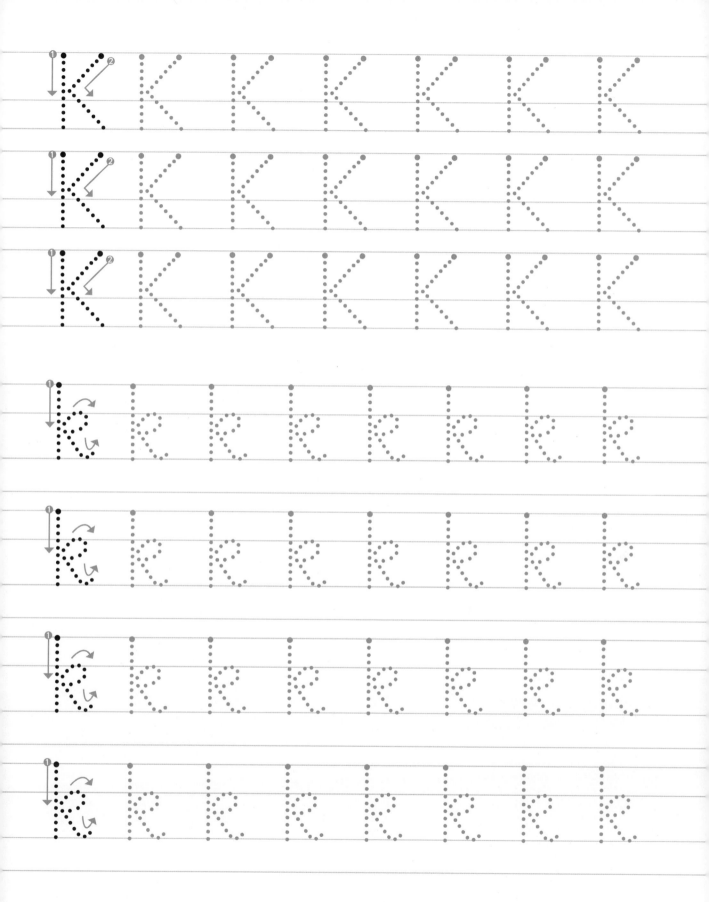

L is for Lion

l is in girl

M is for Mouse

m is in worm

N is for Nurse

n is in sun

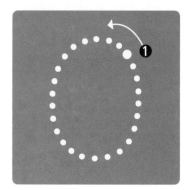

O is for Octopus

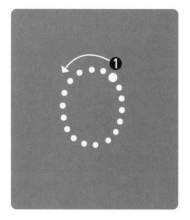

o is in socks

P is for Puppy

p is in sheep

Q is for Queen

q is in squirrel

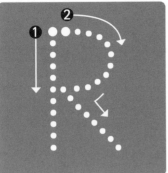

R is for Robot

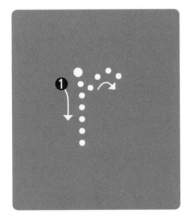

r is in car

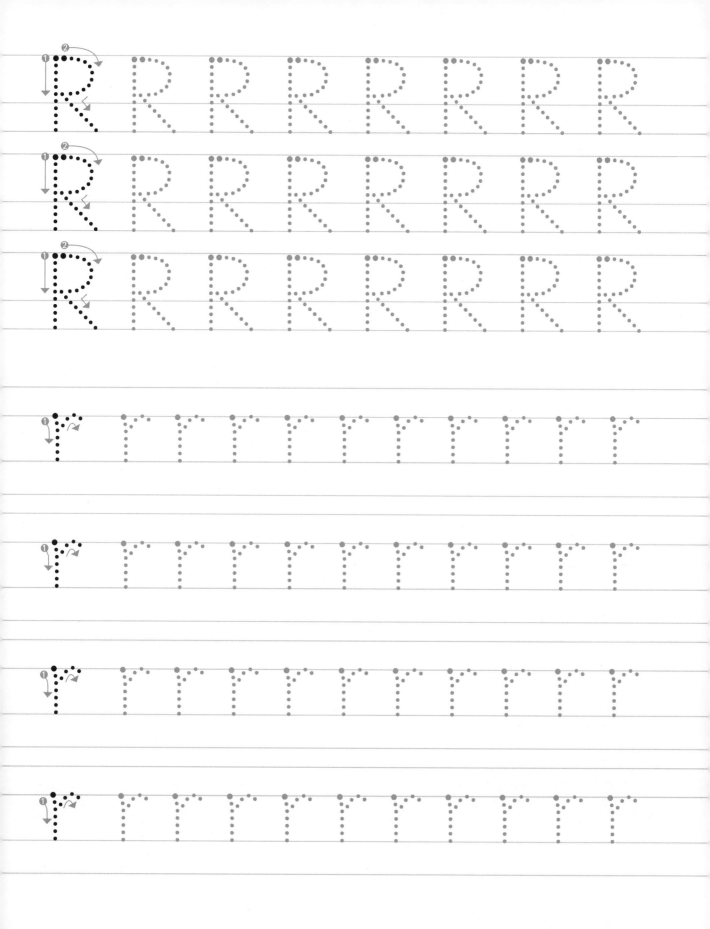

S is for Snake

s is in wasp

S S S S S S S S

S S S S S S S S

S S S S S S S S

S S S S S S S S S S

S S S S S S S S S S

S S S S S S S S S S

S S S S S S S S S S

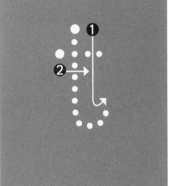

T is for Tiger

t is in bats

T T T T T T T T T

T T T T T T T T T

T T T T T T T T T

t t t t t t t t t

t t t t t t t t t

t t t t t t t t t

t t t t t t t t t

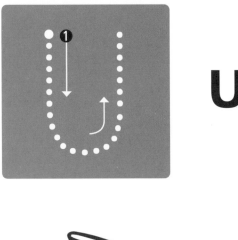

U is for Unicorn

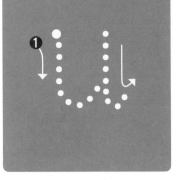

u is in buttercup

U U U U U U U U

U U U U U U U U

U U U U U U U

u u u u u u u u

u u u u u u u u

u u u u u u u u

u u u u u u u u

V is for Volcano

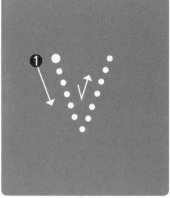

v is in dove

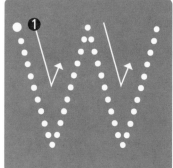

W is for Watch

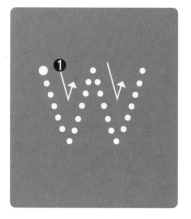

w is in cow

W w

W W W W W W W W

W W W W W W W W

W W W W W W W W

w w w w w w w

w w w w w w w

w w w w w w w

w w w w w w w

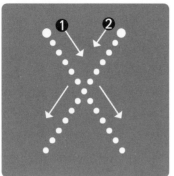

X is for X-ray

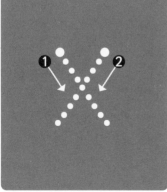

x is in box

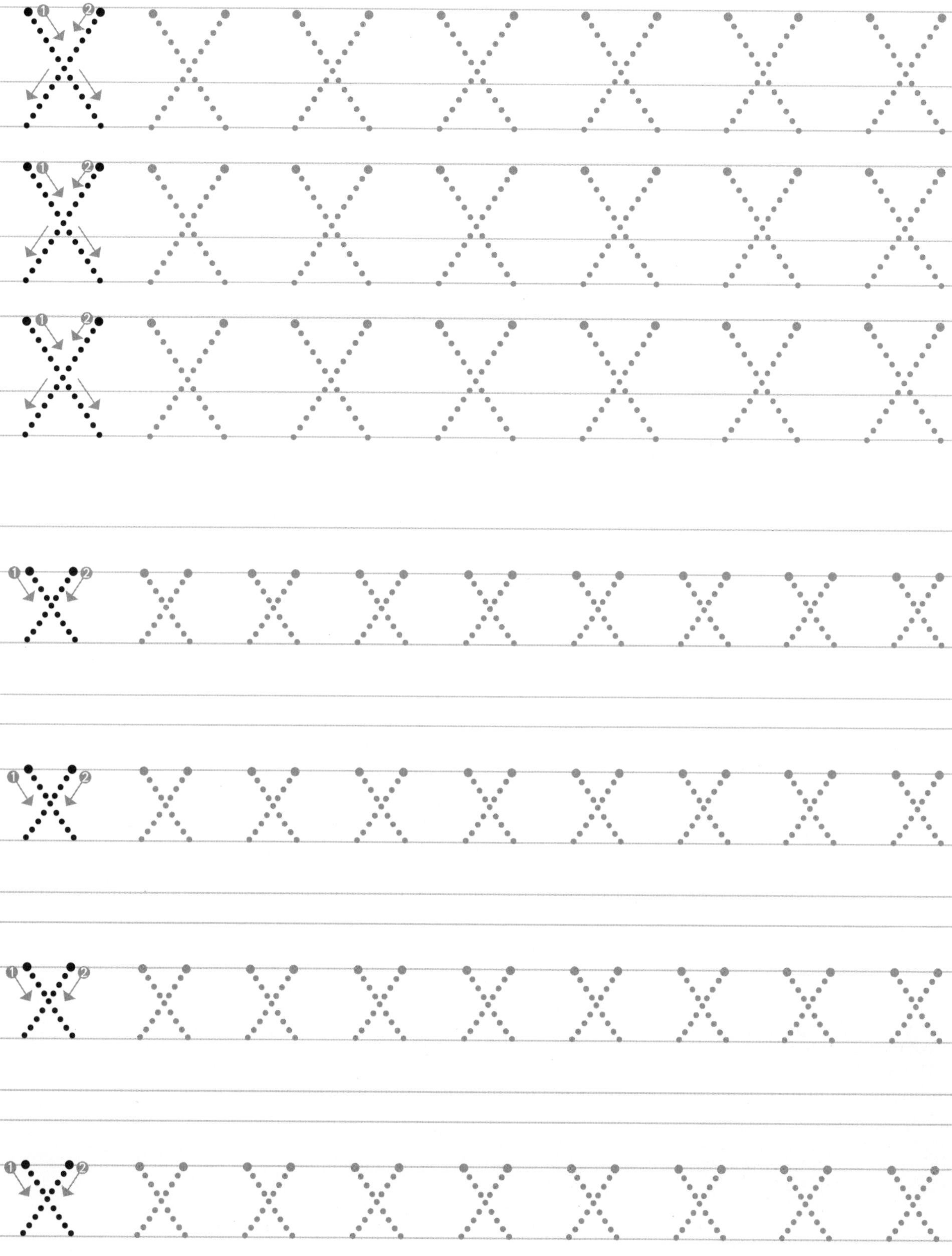

Y is for Yo-yo

y is in boy

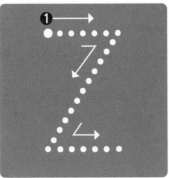

Z is for Zebra

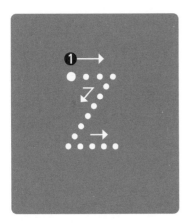

z is in maze

Practice the letter **A**

Aa Aa Aa Aa

Aa Aa Aa Aa

Aa Aa Aa Aa

Aa Aa Aa Aa

Aa Aa Aa Aa

Aa Aa Aa Aa

Practice the letter **B**

Practice the letter **C**

Practice the letter **D**

Practice the letter **E**

Practice the letter **F**

Practice the letter **G**

Practice the letter **H**

Practice the letter **I**

Practice the letter **J**

Practice the letter **K**

Practice the letter **L**

Practice the letter **M**

Practice the letter **N**

Practice the letter O

Practice the letter P

Practice the letter **Q**

Practice the letter **R**

Practice the letter **S**

Practice the letter T

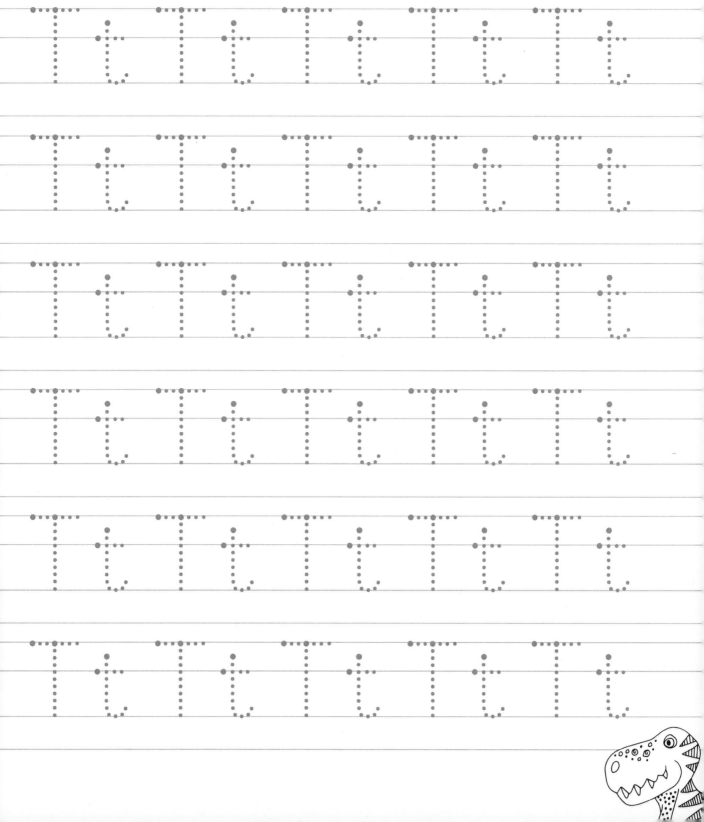

Practice the letter U

Practice the letter **V**

Practice the letter **W**

Practice the letter X

Practice the letter **Y**

Practice the letter Z

Copy the dinosaur word

T-Rex

T-Rex

T-Rex

T-Rex

T-Rex

T-Rex

T-Rex

T-Rex

T-Rex

T-Rex

T-Rex

T-Rex

Copy the dinosaur word

Triceratops

Triceratops

Triceratops

Copy the dinosaur word

Stegosaurus

Stegosaurus

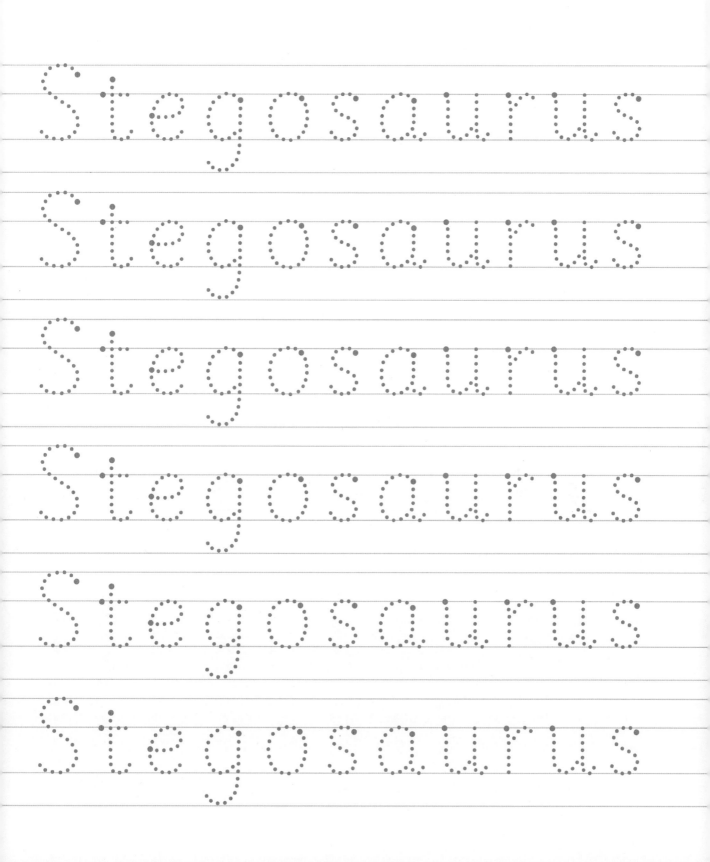

Copy the dinosaur word

Spinosaurus

Spinosaurus

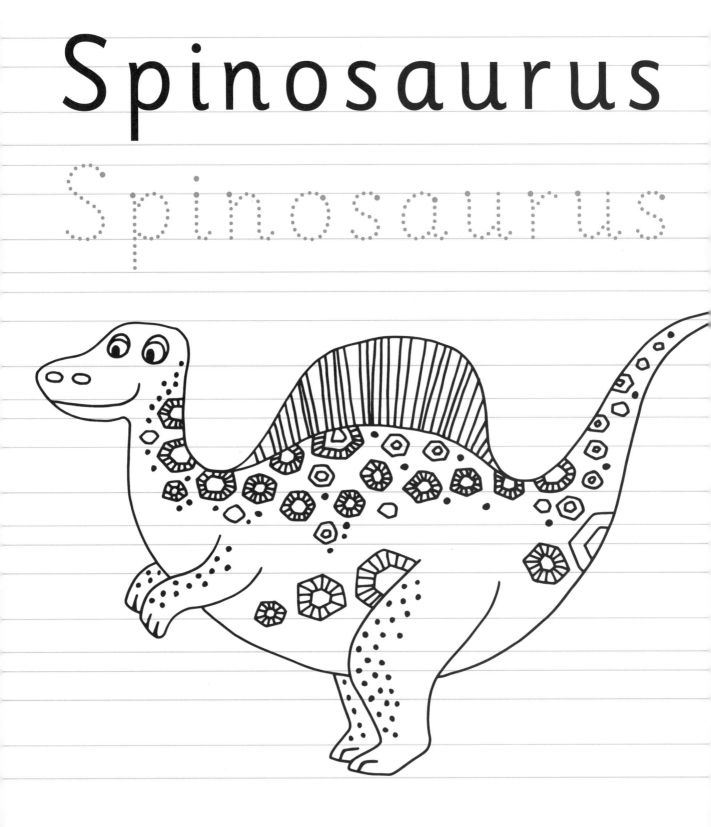

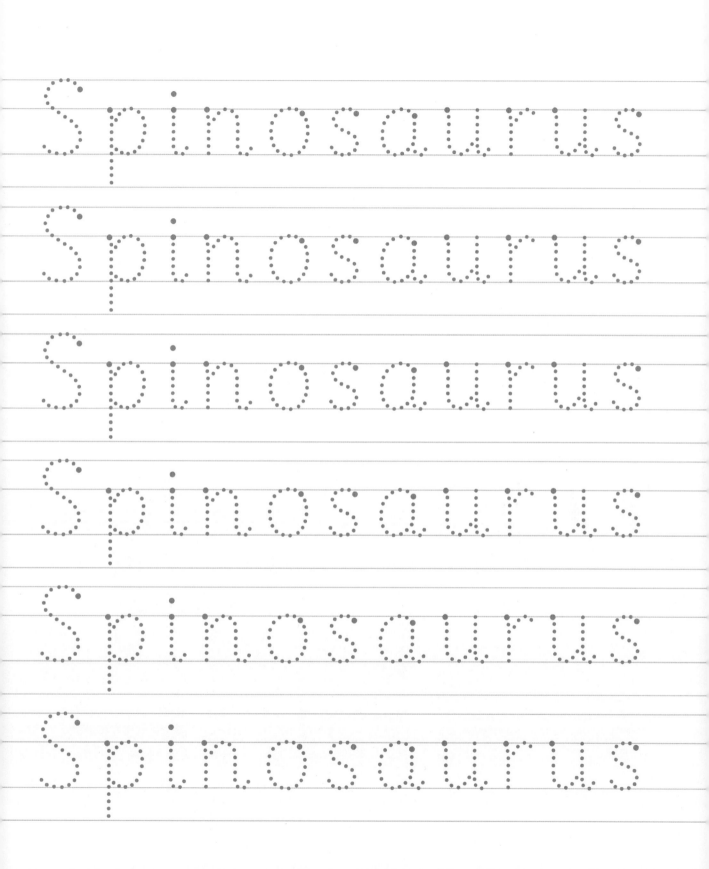

Copy the dinosaur word

Pterodactyl

Pterodactyl

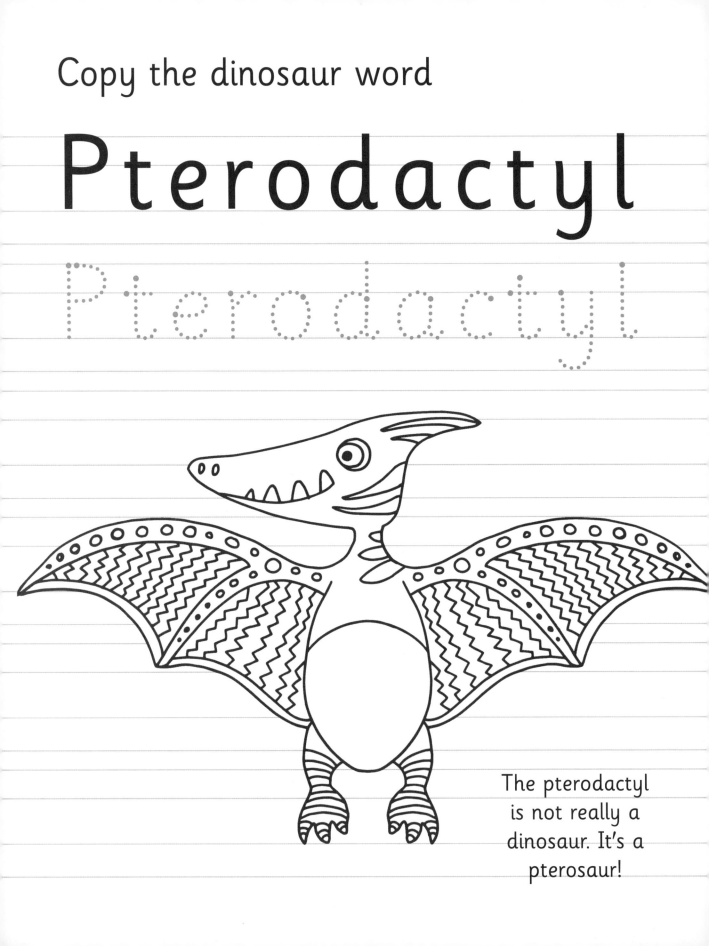

The pterodactyl is not really a dinosaur. It's a pterosaur!

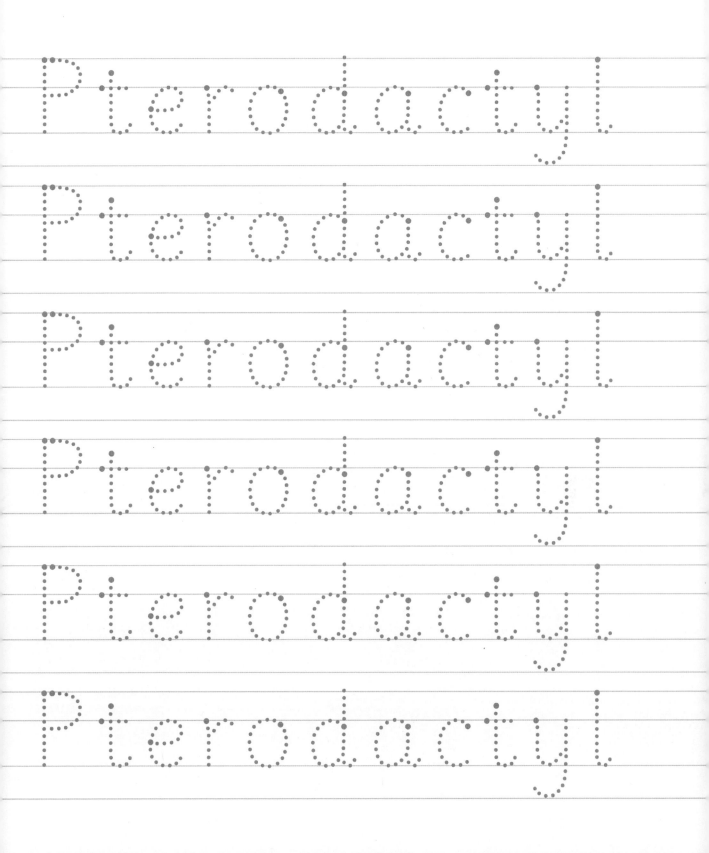

Copy the dinosaur word

Velociraptor

Velociraptor

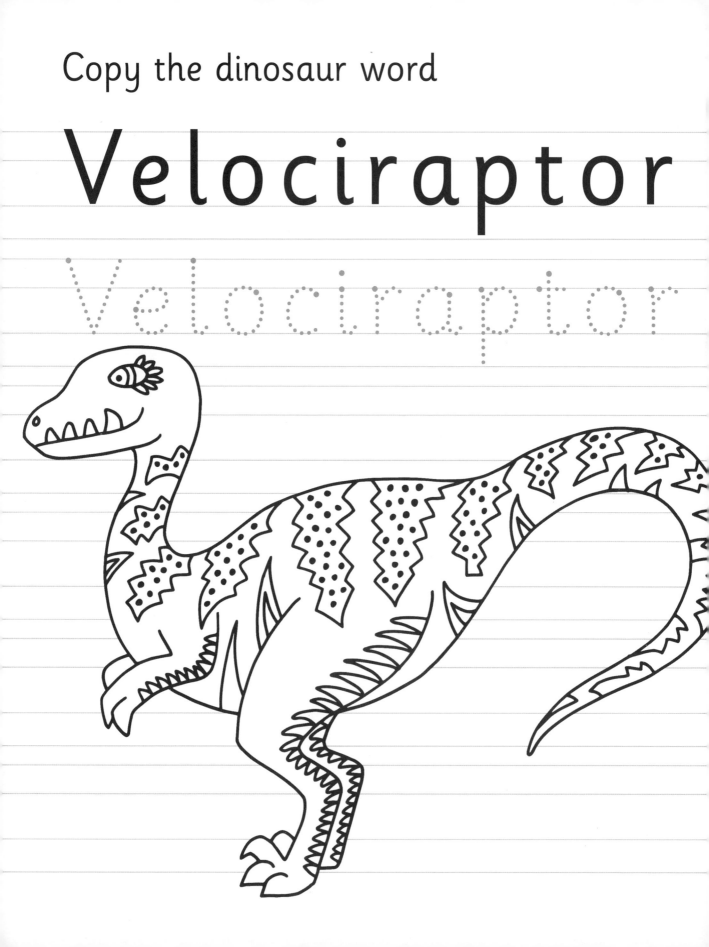

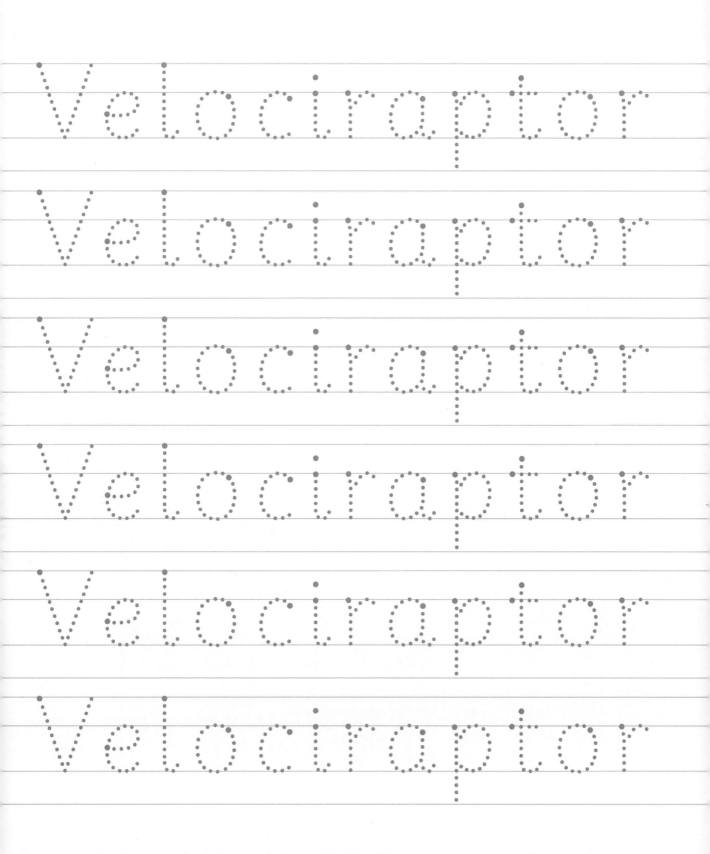

Copy the dinosaur word

Brontosaurus

Brontosaurus

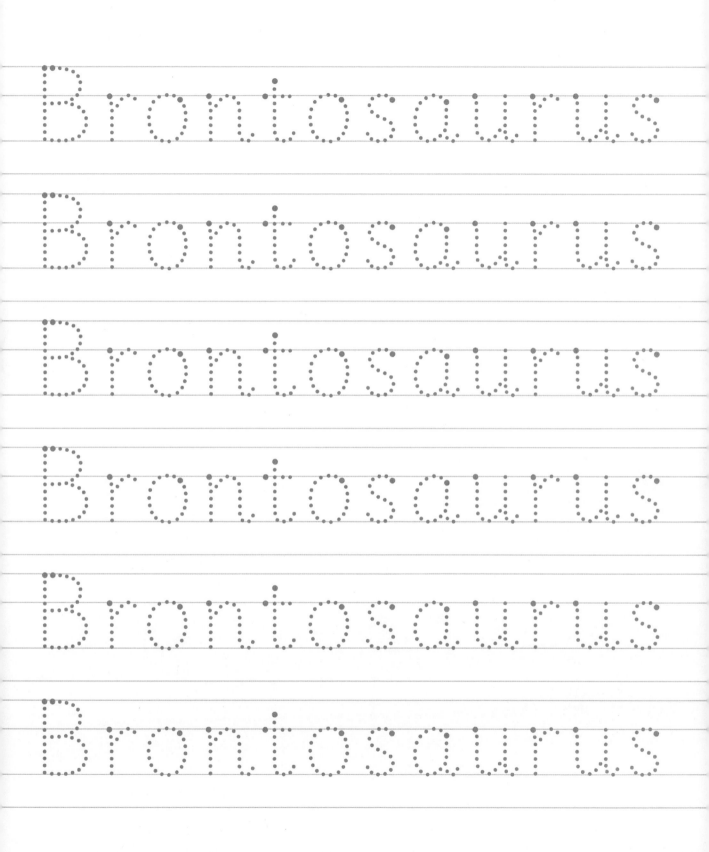

Write the alphabet